Alsace Travel Guide

Sightseeing, Hotel, Restaurant & Shopping Highlights

Emily Sutton

Copyright © 2014, Astute Press
All Rights Reserved.

No part of this publication may be reproduced, stored in a retrieval system, or transmitted, in any form or by any means without the prior written permission of the publisher, nor be otherwise circulated in any form of binding or cover other than that in which it is published and without similar condition being imposed on the subsequent purchaser.

If there are any errors or omissions in copyright acknowledgements the publisher will be pleased to insert the appropriate acknowledgement in any subsequent printing of this publication.

Although we have taken all reasonable care in researching this book we make no warranty about the accuracy or completeness of its content and disclaim all liability arising from its use

Table of Contents

Strasbourg & the Alsace Region 5
Culture 7
Location & Orientation 9
Climate & When to Visit 10

Sightseeing Highlights 11
Strasbourg 11
Kammerzell House 17
Strasbourg Cathedral 17
Hunspach 19
Mont Sainte Odile 20
Colmar 21
Château du Haut-Koenigsbourg 23
Mulhouse 24
Palais Rohan 25
Alsace Wine Route 27

Recommendations for the Budget Traveller 30
Places to Stay 30
Hotel Kyriad Mulhouse Centre 30
Hotel des Vosges 31
Aux Trois Roses 32
Ciarus 33
Hotel du Rhin 33
Places to Eat & Drink 34
Au Koïfhus 34
Zum Strissel 35
Au Tire-Bouchon 35
Le P'tit Cuny 36
Places to Shop 37
Christmas Shopping in Strasbourg 37
La Fromagerie Saint-Nicolas 38
Bookworm 38
Atac Supermarket 39
Chamonix 40

Strasbourg & the Alsace Region

Alsace (Pronounced Al-zass) is one of the smallest and most densely populated provinces in France. Located in the upper east corner of the country, Alsace shares its borders with Germany and Switzerland. The Upper Rhine River cuts across its eastern border and the Vosges Mountains lie to the west.

The word Alsace is derived from an Old High German word meaning "foreign dominion." It's an apt word for this small parcel of land. From as far back as the Roman Empire, Alsace has found itself an unwitting pawn in the game of empire building. Great armies have swept across this land in search of the treasures and wealth found in Paris. WWII was particularly destructive as many of its priceless cathedrals and castles were destroyed.

This tug-of-war resulted in Alsace effectively becoming its own region within the Republic of France. Its capitol, Strasbourg, is a hub of political activity. Dozens of international organizations are based here making it the one of the most important regions within the European Union.

The country is quite small. It is 190 km long and 50 km wide. Packed within this tiny area are nearly 2 million people.

The region has always been known for its fine wine. Roman soldiers returning from this area spoke highly of the quality of wine they found here. Today wine remains one of the top reasons visitors flock to this area. The 'Route de Vin' is a small road that connects the wineries and vineyards with cities and towns.

Alsace is a particularly beautiful part of Europe. Castles and ruins dot the hillsides. Though heavily damaged, the towns retain the old European look and feel lost in so many contemporary cities. Given its history as a stepping-stone to lands beyond, tourists will find nearly as much German influence as French. Restaurants serve some of the finest sauerkraut and beer found outside of Germany.

Alsace has much for the tourist to do. In addition to wine tasting, the picturesque countryside makes for delightful sightseeing and day trips. Many excellent museums are here detailing the history of this area. The food is diverse and particularly good.

Alsace is a unique pocket of Europe.

Culture

The history of this area is one of seemingly endless struggle. Nomadic hunters roamed this area in pre-historic times. In 56 B.C. Romans settled here and began making precious wine it would ship back to Rome to be consumed by the nobles and elite. As the Roman Empire collapsed, the Holy Roman Empire took its place where it remained a seat of power until the Protestant revolution of the 16th century.

Always in the crosshairs of the marauding armies of France, Spain, Holland and Germany, the Alsace region came under French control in 1639.

By the 18th century, Alsatians were expressing a similar discontent and desire for autonomy and self-rule as the people of surrounding France were. When word reached Alsace that the walls of Paris's hated Bastille prison had been broached and citizens seized control, riots broke out and eventually the grip of feudalism overthrown.

Throughout the first half of the 20th century Alsace bounced between German and French control. Following WWII the region was taken over by France in whose hands it remains today.

For most of its history Alsatian was spoken. This is a language similar to the German spoken in Switzerland. Today French is the dominant language.

The Germanic influence is most notable in the old style architecture and food. While newer construction is entirely French, the older sections look very much like an old town in Germany. Fires were a frequent occurrence during the time of the bubonic plague. In order to facilitate the construction and reconstructions of homes, houses were made of timber framing and the floors were made of stone. Timber framed houses are also easy to knock down and reconstruct. This was particularly helpful in the past as the Rhine was subject to frequent flooding.

Alsatians are well known lovers of food. German influenced meals dominate the menus. A particular favorite is a form of sauerkraut known as Chouroute. When you visit Alsace be sure to leave your dieting at home as the meals here are notoriously plentiful.

The German influence is also evident in the region's libations. The area is well known for its white wines especially the dry Rieslings. Hops are grown in the northern part of the country and many fine breweries are found throughout the country, particularly around Strasbourg.

Given its turbulent history, Alsace has taken on symbolic importance as a place of hope where pan-European alliances can be formed. In 1949 Strasbourg became the seat of the Council of Europe. Today the European Parliament is here.

Alsatians are known as warm and convivial people. Their joie de vivre is particularly evident during the holidays which they celebrate with great enthusiasm. Their welcoming spirit is a delight for travelers looking for a place to slow down and relax a bit. If you're looking for beautiful scenery you can explore while dining on fine food and wine, Alsace may be just what you're looking for.

http://www.region-alsace.eu/region-alsace/discovering-alsace-region

Location & Orientation

France consists of 27 regions. Alsace is the fifth smallest. Alsace lies slightly south and to the east of Paris at a distance of 379 km (235 miles). Across its southern border is the Swiss city of Basil. 456 km (283 miles) directly east of Colmar is Munich Germany.

Travelling to and around Alsace is quite easy. Major roads link the area to the rest of France as well as Germany and Switzerland. Europe's fine rail network links the region with the whole of Europe and beyond. Tourists can also arrive on a boat running the Rhine River. Alsace is the most cycle friendly area of France. 2000 km (1242 miles) of bike paths crisscross the countryside. Three EuroVelo routes pass through the area.

Climate & When to Visit

Winters are notoriously harsh in Alsace. Thanks to the nearby Vosges Mountains, very little snow and rain falls here. Winter highs range between 4-6 c (40-47 f). Nights will fluctuate between -0.1 and -0.3 c (30-33f). Spring months find the days ranging between 11 and 20 c (52-68 f) and nights vary between 2 and 9c (36-49f). Summers are mostly sunny and the daytime temperatures fall between 20-25c (68-77f). Nighttime hovers between 12-14c (55-58f). The start of fall finds the daytime temperatures starting at 21c (69f), and falling to 5c (41f) in December. Nights start at 10c (51f) and will drop to 0.3c (32f) when winter starts.

Sightseeing Highlights

Strasbourg

http://www.otstrasbourg.fr/?lang=en

Located in the Eastern part of the Alsace region near the German border is the capital city of Strasbourg. Given the changing political fortunes of the area, Strasbourg has long been a prized pawn. Strasbourg itself is a French and Germanic name. Stras is derived from the German Strasse, or street.

Bourg is a French word which means Burg in German and borough in English. Strasbourg roughly means the 'fortress on the street.' This harkens back to a time when the city was of exceeding geographic and economic importance. Goods traded between the east and western parts of Europe had to pass through the fortification of Strasbourg.

In addition to being the seat of the European Parliament, Strasbourg also hosts numerous other European institutions including the European Court of Human Rights, the European Ombudsman of the European Union and the Central Commission for Navigation of the Rhine.

In 1988 UNESCO classified the entire city center as a historic city Center. This was the first time in history UNESCO bestowed the honor on an entire city.

Every the hybrid of French and German cultures, this coexistence extends to its tolerance of religions as well. The city plays host to a large number of people of the Catholic and Protestant faith. In November 20012 the Strasbourg Grand Mosque opened. It is the largest Mosque in France.

In addition to the beauty found in the Alsace region, Strasbourg is within easy distance of some spectacular scenery. The city lies on the Upper Rhine River Basin along the Ill River. Across the border in Germany, the Ill flows into the Rhine. 25 km (16 miles) to the west is Germany's beautiful Black Forest. This Black Forest is so named because it thick carpet of conifers block out all of the sunlight.

The forest is renowned for its many hiking and biking trails. Deep within the forest the headwaters of the Danube can be found. Cutting across its hills are the continental divide. On its western side water will flow into the Rhine River and out to the Atlantic Ocean. On the eastside water will flow into the Danube and empty into the Black Sea. Within easy driving distance from Strasbourg are found some of Europe's finer examples of old cities that date back hundreds of year. Among these are Staufen, Haslach, Calw and Freiburg.

Wine connoisseurs who want to take a break from tasting French wines will find a wonderful tour running from the south to the north of the Black Forest. Perhaps the greatest exports to come out of this region are its clocks. The clock making industry somewhat died out following the first and second world wars but these legendary clocks are still on display. A circular route that takes you around the forest stops in all the little towns where the craft of clock making was turned into an art. The clock tour is not often on the radar of many tourists, which is a pity. They are really quite amazing and worth the time to take the tour.

 20 km (12 miles) to the west are the Vosges Mountains. With Switzerland so nearby, calling the Vosges 'mountains' might be a bit of a stretch. They are more like the undulating hills found in the nearby Black Forest. Of particular interest is the Northern Vosges Regional Natural Park. Listed by UNESCO as one of world's international biosphere reserves, the park is one of those places of untouched beauty.

All manner of forest and fauna are found here. Numerous animals including deer and lynx call the park home. 1,650 km of hiking and biking trails crisscross the park. In an area of such unique beauty, the park stands out as a particular favorite for tourists visiting the area.

The Vosges Mountains were one of the most contested areas during WWI. This annexed area was a matter of national pride for France. In 1914 both armies dug in and waged a war for possession of this parcel of land that lasted over a year. The battle effectively resulted in a standoff. Each side dug itself ever deeper into the ground by building enormous trenches and encampments dug into the granite. Remains of these can be found to this day.

The city itself is often considered one of the most beautiful in the world. Within the city are numerous attractions to delight the tourist with some of the finest attractions found in Europe.

One of the favorite walks is through a neighborhood known as Le Petite France. Known as the French Quarter, this is a city that remains as it was when built during the middle ages. As you walk among its cobblestones you can take in an ancient city that is all but lost as progress marches on. This is a high rent section of town. It is where you will find the finest dining the city has to offer as well elegant shopping.

The Musée Alsacien or Alsatian Museum located on 23-25 quai Saint-Nicolas, is dedicated preserving artifacts from pre and early industrial Alsace. This an excellent place to visit if you want to get an idea of what life was life in simpler times.

An interesting garden is the Botanical Gardens located at 28 Rue Goethe. Unlike the well-manicured gardens found in Japan or Victoria B.C., Strasbourg's Botanical Gardens are somewhat overgrown and left to nature to cultivate as she sees fit. Because of this the garden plays host to not only a large variety of plants but is home to numerous insects and amphibians as well.

Amid a city of cobblestone streets and medieval architecture sits the ultra-modern European Parliament. Located at Allee du Printemps, the building is quite noticeable from far away. Visitors are welcome when Parliament is in session. If you wish to see this, be sure to plan your trip accordingly. The website is www.europarl.europa.eu/ Once there you must call ahead to assure yourself a seat. The phone number is 33 (0)3 88 17 20 07

Another art museum that is a favorite for visitors to Strasbourg is the Musee des Beaux-Arts. Taken from a poem by W.H. Auden and translated as the Museum of Fine Arts, the museum houses one of the largest collections of art by the Dutch painter, Pieter Bruegel the Elder. What are most appreciated by visitors are the detailed explanations that accompany the works of art. Rather than featuring a name, title and date, works here are accompanied by explanations of the work, its meaning and its place in the larger context of the times in which they were painted. The museum is located at 2, place du Chateau.

Later will be an explanation of a wine tour you can take around the Alsace region. But if you're in Strasbourg and looking for a place to start your excursion, the Wine cellar of Strasbourg city Hospital is an excellent place to visit. Located in the basement of the city's hospital at 1, Place de l'Hopital, the wine cellar has been in use for over 600 years.

The wine cellar does not advertise itself and can be a bit difficult to find. To find it go to the medical hospital at the Civil Hospital. When you're there walk through the main gate and the entrance will be the first door on your left. You are free to visit it at your leisure. Tours are also available that will give you a good idea on what types of wine you will find around the region. If you would like a tour, call ahead at 33 3 88 11 64 50 to find out when they are available.

One final attraction in the city itself that will give you a good idea of the history of the area is the Musee Archeologique , Strasbourg's Archeological Museum. Located at 2, place du Chateau, the museum is an old style museum that looks like a gothic cathedral. Headsets are available to will walk you through the exhibits. Here you will find excellent examples extending back as far as the Neolithic and Roman occupation. Other works follow the history of the area right up to the present day. If you're spending a night or two in Strasbourg before heading out to explore the countryside, a visit to this museum will give you a good idea of the places you will be visiting and its history.

Kammerzell House

16 Place Cathedrale, Strasbourg
+33 3 88 32 42 14
http://www.maison-kammerzell.com/accueil_en.php

The Kammerzell House sits atop what was the headquarters for the Holy Roman Empire. First built in 1427, the building went through renovations in 1467 and 1589; it remains a masterpiece of German Renaissance architecture. The house was for civil purposes. Because of this it was constructed in the traditional black and white timber framed style.

The interior, with its sumptuous display of frescos by Leo Schnug is on display to the public. The house now features a restaurant.

Strasbourg Cathedral

Place de la Cathedrale
67000
Strasbourg, France
+33 3 88 32 75 78
http://www.strasbourg.info/cathedral/

Known as the Cathedral of Our Lady of Strasbourg, construction on the cathedral began in 1015 and was completed in 1439. Over the years poets and writers have marveled at it beauty. Victor Hugo called it a "gigantic and delicate marvel." Goethe, with his better sense of poetry, called it a "sublimely towering, wide-spreading tree of God."

At 142 m (466 feet) was the tallest cathedral in the world until it was superseded St. Nikolai's Church in Hamburg Germany. Today it remains the sixth tallest cathedral in the world. So tall is it that it can be seen across the entire planes of Alsace. Its spire is visible from the Vosges Mountains in France on into the Black forest in Germany.

Throughout history the land upon which the cathedral sits has been used as a place of worship for a number of different religions. The Roman emperor Nero Claudius Drusus established a military outpost across the Rhine River. On the site of Strasbourg Cathedral his army made camp calling the area Argentoratum. Over the years this place burned six times. The emperor Trajan laid the foundations upon which the modern church sits was first established.

Over the years construction has continued. Each successive building built on the last but added modern touches to the building. A walk around the cathedral gives a fascinating glimpse into the various architectural styles that have gone into its construction. Along its southern transept are found examples of 13th century statues and sculptures. Of particular interest is the 'Pillar of Angels' featuring a depiction of the Last Judgment.

Around the cathedral is evidence of its Romanesque style. Later cathedrals would place great emphasis on high windows with colored glass depicting biblical scenes. The Strasbourg Cathedral features much more ornate and intricate walls than those found on newer ones. Of particular interest is the west front. Carved in the Gothic period, thousands of scenes and figures are carved into its walls.

It is a stunning testament to the ingenuity and craftsmanship of Gothic artists. It cannot fail to move anyone with even a passing interest in art. For a religious person it seems divinely inspired and is a place of veneration and worship.

Like all great works of art, Strasbourg Cathedral has been a beacon to those of ill intent. In June of 1940, Hitler visited this spoil of war and declared it to be a shrine for the German people. Later the stained glass windows were removed and hidden in a salt mine in Heilbronn Germany. In August of 1944, British and American bombers carpetbombed the area with the intent of driving the Germans out of France. The Cathedral sustained significant damage that was not fully repaired until the late 1990's. More recent times have seen a cell of Al-Qaeda bombers intent on blowing up the cathedral and a nearby Christmas market, broken up by French and German police.

Hunspach

http://www.tourisme-alsace.com/en/272000057-Hunspach.html

This beautiful little town is located in the North Vosges Natural Park. The German influence is very much in evidence here as the houses are built in the Alsatian half-timbered style. Primarily a farming community, Hunspach is one of those delightful European villages that exist nowhere else in the world. Hunspach is frequently referred to as one of the most beautiful villages in France.

Mont Sainte Odile

http://www.mont-sainte-odile.com/?lang=en

Named after Saint Odile, daughter of Adalrich, Duke of Alsace, this spectacular monastery/convent sits atop a 760 m (2500 foot) peak in the Vosges Mountains.

This site has been a place of veneration and worship for as long as humans have occupied the area. Evidence of Neolithic and Celtic settlements has been found in the surrounding area. The Romans used the site to construct a strategically placed fortress from which they could look down upon invading armies. In 407 their luck ran out as Vandals overran the fortress and leveled it to the ground. By the 10th century most Europeans had converted to Christianity. It was then that Vikings attacked and swept across the Low Countries. The seat of power for church officials and bishops at that time was in Utrecht. Sensing a grim future, the bishops fled in exile and took up residence at Mont Sainte Odile. The building was destroyed during the Middle Ages and rebuilt in the 17th century.

One of the great works of Christian literature the Hortus Deliciarum or Garden of Delights was written and illustrated by Herrad of Landsberg was written here in the 12th century when it was known as the Hohenburg Abbey. At its time it was a veritable encyclopedia of all that was known.

One of the more notable features of Mont Sainte Odile is the 'Pagan Wall.' Why and when it was built is a matter of some dispute. It seems undeniable that the wall was constructed as a way of keeping marauding invaders at bay. The structure circles Mont Sainte Odile at a length of 10 kilometers (6.2 miles) at a height of 3 meters (9.8 feet) high and a width of 1.8 meters (5 feet 11 inches). Legend has it that the wall was originally constructed by Druids more than 3,000 years ago. Of late, scholars date its construction to the 7th century and attribute its name 'Pagan Wall' to Pope Leo IX.

Colmar

Colmar is another of those uniquely beautiful cities in the Alsace region that deserves a visit. It is one of the stops on the wine tasting tour that will be discussed in a bit. If you're not making a wine tour the city makes for a relaxing day stroll.

Located between Strasbourg and Basel, Colmar is a medieval town that has preserved much of the architecture and charm from those times. While some recent construction has gone on, the old town has remained intact and is where you will find all of its attractions.

Of all its old buildings none is more beautiful than the Maison des Tetes or House of Heads. This wooden house was built during the Renaissance. Now a hotel, the Maison is best known for its interesting carvings of faces and heads that adorn the building's façade.

Nearby is the St. Martian Church. What makes this church so interesting is that it is colored pink. Visitors to the Strasbourg Cathedral will have noticed that a part of its exterior is also pink. The color of the stone is found only in a particular spot in the nearby mountains.

Lying at the entrance New York City's harbor is the Statue of Liberty. What most people don't realize is that the statue was a gift from the French. The sculpture of the iconic American statue was a man from Colmar named Frédéric Auguste Bartholdi. In Colmar there is a museum named the Bartholdi Museum that is dedicated to his life and work.

Of particular pride for the citizens of Colmar is the Unterlinden Museum (http://www.musee-unterlinden.com/). The museum houses a unique collection of Alsatian art. In addition to paintings, the museum has an exquisite collection various types of furniture and everyday household items used by Alsatians of years past. Also found are paintings by Renoir, Holbein the Elder and Picasso.

Little Venice is a collection of canals found in the old part of Colmar. In times past the canals were the way produce and goods were ferried around the city. Today a scenic boat ride along the canals is a relaxing and unique way to view the medieval charm of Colmar.

Château du Haut-Koenigsbourg

67600 Orschwiller, France
+33 3 69 33 25 00
http://www.haut-koenigsbourg.fr/en

Here is another stop on the wine route that is well worth a visit by itself. The chateau sits high in the Vosges Mountains and commands a sweeping view of Alsatian plain. When it was first built is unknown. The first references to it are found in the 12th century.

In this land of such strategic importance, the little spur of land upon which the chateau sits has been a hotly contested bit of real estate. During the Thirty Years War the chateau was overrun by the Swedish army who ransacked and all but destroyed it. Its obvious beauty and haunting ruins were the inspiration for many of the leading romantic poets and painters.

On the eve of the 18th century, Bodo Ebhardt was commissioned with the task of rebuilding the castle to what it was prior to the Thirty Years War. Using what plans he could find, Ebhardt worked for 8 years to restoring it to its former glory. He did his job exceedingly well and the chateau has remained one of the most popular tourist sites in France. In 1993 the French Ministry of Culture designated it as a national historic site.

Mulhouse

http://www.mulhouse.fr/en/

Mulhouse is the second largest city in the Alsace region behind Strasbourg. Located in the eastern part of the region it's close to the borders of Switzerland and Germany.

Its founding is unsure. The earliest written record of its existence dates from the 12th century. The city itself is steeped in myth. Local legends tell of a city dating back to the first century B.C. At the height of the French Revolution the Treaty of Mulhouse was signed and control of the city was taken over by France until the Franco-Prussian War of 1870. At that time it came under German rule as part of the Alsace-Lorraine territory. The city essentially remained in German hands until the area was returned to France in May 1945.

Industry in Mulhouse consisted mainly of textiles. Throughout the 19th century the city enjoyed a lively trade with the state of Louisiana. Bales of cotton poured into the city fueling its burgeoning textile industry. Later the city would become a hub for engineering and textile industries. Today it has branched to electronics and automobiles. The largest employer in Alsace is the Peugeot factory in Mulhouse.

The city is divided into four districts. The Rebberg district was built on the wealth of Louisiana cotton. Originally this was the heart of wine production. Rebbe is German for 'Vine.' The layout of the town was constructed to resemble that of Manchester England with houses built on terraced steppes.

The Nouveau Quarter (New District) is the expensive part of the city. After the stone walls were torn down in 1826, work began on developing a carefully orchestrated layout for the city. The precision of its streets are a model that should serve as a template for cities built today.

The Lower Town is where the artists, craftsmen and merchants are to be found. This area is for pedestrians only and makes for a delightful walk and day of shopping.

The Upper Town has been under construction for 300 years now. This part of the city is where the majority of religious institutions are located. Many monasteries are found here. Throughout the years this section has hosted Augustinians, Franciscans, Knights of Malta and Poor Clares.

Palais Rohan

2 Place du Chateau,
67000 Strasbourg
+33 3 88 52 50 00
http://www.musees.strasbourg.eu/index.php?page=le-palais-rohan-en

The Palais Rohan, or Rohan palace, is one of the more interesting sites in all of Alsace. In an area known for it rich and varied architecture, Palais Rohan stands alone. Built in the early part of the 18th century, it is a masterpiece of Baroque architecture. Commissioned by by the King's architect Robert de Cotte, the building first served as the residence of Cardinal Armand-Gaston de Rohan-Soubise, Prince Bishop of Strasbourg.

Its style was to mimic and one up the Parisian homes of the wealthy and elite. Through the years other notables have taken up residence here. King Louis XV stayed here in the middle of the century, while the ill-fated Marie Antoinette lived there in 1770. Napoleon Bonaparte lived here in the early years of the 19th century and added some rooms for his comfort and that of his wife.

Today the building is noted for its collection of museums. In its basement is the Archeological museum. The ground floor hosts the Museum of Decorative Arts. On its first floor is the Fine Arts Museum.

Even if you've become a bit weary of museums by the time you reach Strasbourg, the building is worth a look. Its high facades and exquisite interior faithfully preserve the time it was built. It looks as if you've stepped into a set of a Hollywood movie - but it is all real. Step inside and realize that this was the residence of many people who occupied it during some of the most turbulent times in French history - it is almost a sublime experience.

Alsace Wine Route

http://www.vinsalsace.com/en/
http://en.wikipedia.org/wiki/File:Weinbau-frankreich-elsass.png

The Alsace Wine Route is one of those famous places not to be missed by connoisseurs of fine wines. In recent years Australia and America have begun producing world-class wines. Tours through the southwest corner of Australia, California and Washington State are a treat of fine wines, good food, comfortable surroundings and convivial company but they lack that certain something a tour through wine's old country has. The vineyards are soaked in history.

You feel the love and craftsmanship of generation's vintners who worked the soil, tending to the grapes through good times and bad, and celebrated their fortunes with friends and family over good meals, much laughter and fine wine. It's also quite amazing to think that Romans took up residence here to grow grapes, produce wine, drink themselves silly as soldiers are want to do, and ship the rest back to Rome where it was consumed by emperors, nobles and statesmen.

Alsatian wine is primarily white wine. The region is particularly famous for its dry Rieslings. Another favorite are the Gewürztraminer wines. Like much else about this region, the wines produced here are heavily influenced by German wines. Wines here are tightly controlled by the Appellation d'Origine Contrôlée or 'controlled designation of origin.'

Three main types are produced. Alsace Grand Cru AOC is for white wines produced at certain locations. Crémant d'Alsace AOC is for sparkling wines. Alsace AOC is for red, rosé and white wines. The wines here tend to be very aromatic. As mentioned earlier, early wine production was influenced by German tastes.

With political and geographic autonomy, wine makers have exhibited a similar zeal to produce wine with a unique Alsatian stamp on them. Initially this led to growers to produce very dry wines. Lately wine makers are producing wines with residual sugar in them. Pinot Gris and Gewürztraminer wines are often produced this way. Muscat, Riesling and Sylvaner wines tend to be much dryer. The Alsace region also produces some excellent desert wines. Because of this, traditional wines may not be quite what you're accustomed to.

Alsace wines are produced along a small strip of land. This topographical map will give you a good idea of the wine country and surrounding terrain:
http://en.wikipedia.org/wiki/File:Alsace_topo.png

The mountains on the west are the Vosges Mountains. Alsace is subjected to westerly winds most of the time. The mountains provide ideal protection from storm fronts passing through that would deluge vineyards with rain. The region ranges between 175-420 meters (600-1,400 feet). With the dry conditions and plentiful sunlight, conditions are ideal for wine production. The best of the wines are produced out of the shadow of the Vosges range on the south-east and south-west slopes.

The wine route of Alsace is called the Route des Vins d'Alsace. This well-marked road runs from north to south. This 170 km road passes through 67 communes. Many more wineries are found along the way. There are so many places to sample wine and have a meal that it would be impossible to do them justice here. While there are favorites that stand out among visitors, it would be impossible to give definitive locations. An excellent website that contains a wonderful map and is stuffed with useful information is: http://www.alsace-wine-route.com/en/alsace-wine-route-and-cycle-route-map/ The bottom line is that this is an area best left for you to explore.

Whether by car or on bicycle, the Route des Vin d'Alsace is a place that rewards the curious. If locals have one bit of advice it is that you avoid the popular spots. By doing so you will find a place much less crowded where you can relax with a glass or two of wine, enjoy a sumptuous meal and take in the breathing beauty of the Alsace region.

Travel rewards the curious and if you take time to explore you will find a number of quaint places just off the beaten path where you had the finest wine, meal, company and views of anywhere you have ever visited. The best advice to visiting this area is to do some homework. Get a feel for the land and its towns, then just get out and explore.

Another option is the many tour companies that will take you to the most popular destinations. Tour companies will take you to the best spots. Knowledgeable guides will inform you of what you are passing along the way. If you do choose a tour company, look around the internet and see how it is rated by those who have used it. This will give you a good idea of its reputation.

Recommendations for the Budget Traveller

Places to Stay

Hotel Kyriad Mulhouse Centre

23, Rue des Trois Frontiers
68111 Illzach
+33 3 89 61 81 50
http://www.kyriad.com/en/hotels/kyriad-mulhouse-nord-illzach

The Kyriad are a chain of three star hotels found throughout France. This particular one is chosen because it lies at the beginning of the wine tour. Mulhouse is one of Alsace's more popular cities and is known for its many museums and tourist attractions.

This hotel has 47 rooms, each with a private bath. 2 rooms are specially designed for people with limited mobility. The hotel has a restaurant and bar. The chef is well known for preparing local meals that are in season.

Its location is ideally suited. The airport is a 20 minute drive away. Major roads intersect in Mulhouse making excursions into Germany and Switzerland quite easy.

Room rates start at 50€.

Hotel des Vosges

3 Place De La Gare
67000 Strasbourg
1-866-539-0066

Conveniently located near the train station, the Hotel des Vosges in been in existence for over 100 years. Much of the hotel is built in the style found in the years just prior to WWI. A particular favorite for travelers is its Breakfast Room. This has the look and feel of an old style Alsatian tavern with a fireplace blazing away. An excellent restaurant is open for all meals.

Within easy walking distance are the Strasbourg Cathedral, the Notre Dame Museum and the Alsatian Museum.

All rooms are smoke free. Dogs are allowed in the rooms. Bathrooms have all necessary amenities. Rooms have a television with cable access. Wireless internet access is available for a surcharge.

Rooms start at 65 €.

Aux Trois Roses

7, Rue de Zurich
67000 Strasbourg
00 33 (0) 3 88 36 56 95
http://hotel3roses-strasbourg.com/UK/index.php

This is a hotel that is preferred by backpackers and travelers who think hotels are a place to drop off you stuff, go out and explore, crash for the night and get up and do it all again. It is a bare bones place with little of the luxuries and comforts found in more expensive hotels.

While it is not the sort of place you would want to spend a few days resting after a bought of sightseeing, it is not a shed either. The Aux Trois Roses has a sauna and a sunken Jacuzzi. A breakfast area serves breakfast for a surcharge. Its 32 rooms feature minibars. All rooms have tubs and showers. Wireless internet access is available. Rooms have a LCD television with satellite connection.

Rooms start at 77€.

Ciarus

7 Rue Finkmatt
F-Strasbourg
+ 33 (0) 3 88 15 27 88
http://www.ciarus.com/

The Ciarus is a hostel located in the center of Strasbourg. It is one of those places that appeals to younger travelers, including the backpack and hitching crowd. It is a loud, noisy boisterous hostel that seems to bustle with activity 24 hours a day. It is a wonderful place to meet travelers who have arrived from all points far and near.

The Ciarus has 290 beds in 101 rooms. Rooms range from single beds to double beds to rooms with bunk beds. All rooms have a private toilet, sink and shower. Wi-Fi internet access is available. The reception area is open 24 hours and has a wealth of material for travelers on their way across Europe.

Rooms start at 21€.

Hotel du Rhin

7, place de la Gare
6700 Strasbourg
+33 3 88 32 35 00
http://hotel-du-rhin.fr/?lang=en

Built during the reign of Kaiser Wilhelm II, this cozy hotel is a steal. Its rooms are tastefully decorated and give a warm feel. Many rooms have excellent views including the new and impossible to describe train station.

The staff is multi-lingual and is available to answer any questions you may have. In addition tours are run from the hotel. If you wish to make a day excursion around the cities and neighboring area or book a wine tour, you can do so at the front desk.

All rooms have a private bath. Wi-Fi internet access is available. Satellite TV is available in all rooms.

Rooms start at 71€.

ALSACE TRAVEL GUIDE

Places to Eat & Drink

Au Koïfhus

2 pl. de l'Ancienne-Douane
Colmar, 68000
03 89 23 04 90
www.restaurant-koifhus-colmar.fr

A well-known spot for locals, this restaurant features traditional meals from the Alsace region. Among its specialties are coq au vin with spaetzle, crayfish and grapefruit salad choucrote colmarienne served with a variety of different meats. A meal should cost between 12 and 15€.

Zum Strissel

5 pl. de la Grande-Boucherie,
Strasbourg 67000
03 88 32 14 73
www.strissel.fr

It's not often you get to eat at a restaurant that first opened its doors in the 1500's. The Zum Strissel is a unique dining experience. The interior is decorated to reflect the rich history of the area. Meals are most traditional fare. Baeckoffe and Choucroute served with pike perch are particular specialties. Its bar is richly stocked with a wide variety of Alsatian wines. If you want dinner in an old-fashioned location where you can relax and sample some of the best wines the area has to offer, the Zum Strissel is a perfect stop.

Meals cost around 15€.

Au Tire-Bouchon

29 rue du Général-de-Gaulle
Riquewihr 68340
03 89 47 91 61
www.riquewihrzimmer.com

One of the most popular places, the Au Tire-Bouchon is frequently filled with customers. If you would like to dine here it is recommended you call ahead to book a table. Meals are authentic with particular attention paid to seasonal game dishes.

This is not fare for those who think of meat as just steak or a hamburger. A seasonal meal also consists of local produce. What makes the Au Tire-Bouchon stand out is its selection of local wines. This may very well be the place where you can sample the widest variety of Alsatian wines.

Meals start at 13€.

Le P'tit Cuny

97 Grand-Rue, Vieille Ville,
Nancy 54000
03 83 32 85 94
www.lepetitcuny.fr

Food here is more from the Lorraine tradition. This is another one of those locations that is constantly stuffed. The tables are placed close together and the atmosphere is constantly busy as wait staff serve customers.

Le P'tit Cuny has a reputation for serving hearty meals at reasonable prices. Traditional meals can be found here as well as such exotic items as foie gras-stuffed pig's trotter and calf's head.

Meals cost around 15€.

Places to Shop

Christmas Shopping in Strasbourg

Legend has it that the first Christmas tree was put on display in Strasbourg. Whether this is true or not is a matter of some debate. What can be said for sure is that the Christmas market in Strasbourg was founded in 1570. It is considered to be the finest Christmas market in all of Europe. Certainly travelers from large cities will be taken aback by the traditional atmosphere with mechanized Santa's and neon lights.

Open from mid-November through December, the Strasbourg Christmas market is not just a place where merchants sell their wares. With the harvest season just ending and the dark days of winter settle in, the market place becomes a festival dedicated to the season. Shoppers can stroll from chalet to chalet sampling freshly baked deserts and libations. Events take place all the time. Singers, bell ringers and puppet shows will delight the entire family. Needless to say every trinket and bauble related to Christmas can be found here. Shopping at Strasbourg's Christmas market is an experience like none other.

La Fromagerie Saint-Nicolas

18, rue Saint-Nicolas
68000 Colmar
+33 (0)3 89 24 90 45
www.fromagerie-st-nicolas.com

Much has been made of the wine produced in this region, and for good reason. What is often overlooked is the high quality of cheese produced here. Of all the cheese makers in the region none is more famous that this one.

Run by the same family for years, their cheese is most likely what you will be served in nearby restaurants and on display at local farmers markets. Travelers recommendations of this shop are plentiful and consistently rate it highly.

Bookworm

3 rue de Pâques Town Station
03 88 32 26 99
www.bookworm.fr

This is not one of those megastores you can get lost in throughout the afternoon. Instead it is an ideal place for a traveler to find books to help orient him to this great region. If you find yourself in the Alsace region and in need of much more detailed information about the land around you, the Bookworm stocks the books that will help you find what you need. Travelers making 'The Grand Tour' and in need of informative books on what lays beyond will find helpful books to plan their trip as they make their way out of Alsace and off to places unknown.

Atac Supermarket

47 rue des Grandes Arcades Grand Iie
Strasbourg

It is not uncommon to come to this area and find themselves somewhat unprepared. Its wide open spaces, many hikes, pleasant vineyards and warm weather just cry out for a picnic. It's not often a traveler will pack a basket, cheese knife, blanket and cork screw opener. If you find yourself in the area and feel the need to spend a romantic afternoon or two taking in the beautiful scenery on a lonely hillside while dining on cheese and wine, you will find what you need at the Atac Supermarket.

Of course you can find all the groceries if you want to stay in and make you meals where you are staying. But what makes this place special is that it caters to the picnicker. If you find yourself wanting to spend an afternoon under the sun enjoying the day, the Atac Supermarket will have the little knick-knacks you need but just couldn't stow in your luggage.

Chamonix

176 Rue Joseph Vallot
74400 Chamonix
00 33 4 50 93 52 73
www.chamshop@hsd3.fr

Chamonix is one of the stops along the world ski tour. It's trendy, upscale clothing is most likely not on the list of places for the budget traveler but if you're in the market for some of the finest ski attire to be found, things that will make you stand out at the slopes next winter, you can do no better to drop into Chamonix's and see if they have what you're looking for.

Printed in Great Britain
by Amazon.co.uk, Ltd.,
Marston Gate.